The BIG Book

Story by **Kathleen Ruckman**   Illustrations by **Bryan Miller**

The Big Book

First Printing April 2002

Printed in the United States of America

ISBN: 0-89051-358-9

Library of Congress: 2001098881

For information write to Master Books,
P.O. Box 726 Green Forest, AR 72638.

Please visit our website for other great titles:
www.masterbooks.net

Dedication

I want to dedicate
The Big Book to my
four children, Mark, Jim,
Julie and Amy, who have
helped me see the big and awe-
some world from a child's perspective
through the years. I want to thank my hus-
and, Tom, for his love and support in my writ-
ing. And to every child...it's a BIG world, but never
too big for God to notice you and to love you.

Some things
in this world
are as big as can be.
You stand on your
tiptoes to help
you to see.

Great
mountains
are huge and so
wide and so tall;
the climbers use
ropes that will
help them not fall.

Redwoods can be near 300 feet high.

They seem to keep growing up into the sky!

The sky
never ends;
it's so high
and so wide!

You watch airplanes fade then they finally hide!

The sky is like ink but
the moon gives it light,
when children dream
dreams and sleep
tight in the
night.

The ocean is mighty;
its waves lap and crash!

When you stand at the edge,
you might just get a splash!

You look at a ship,
and it seems very tall,

But on the vast ocean the ship's really small!

Sometimes from the
seashore you might see a hump —
A large lumpy, bumpy, humongous gray lump!

It must be a whale and he's big as can be!
He makes a big splash as he jumps in the sea!

Colossal sized animals
lived on the land.
A really big dinosaur
simply was grand!

His tail was as long as his neck and oh my!
The earth felt a thump when this giant walked by!

In parks you can somersault, roll, romp, and run,

And you can throw Frisbees far into the sun!

Some people are massive, so strong and so quick;
They get to the goal line — lickety-split!

Yes
God made
everything,
mighty and
few.

He made some things large and
He also made YOU!